INTRODUCTION

THE BRETON

by

Wendy Mewes

979-10-90374-09-6

Published by
Red Dog Books, 29690 Berrien, France
email: reddogbooks@orange.fr
www.reddogbooks.com

Dépôt légal: octobre 2019
Diffusion par Coop Breizh

———————————— o ————————————

CONTENTS

Cover illustrations
front: *St Thélo, Chapelle de Kerdévot (photo courtesy of Gaëlle Martin at Ergué-Gabéric)*
back: *St Samson (Dol cathedral), St Gildas (Carnoët), St Miliau (Guimiliau), St Noyale (Sainte-Noyale)*

Lanmeur, the crypt

God guided the small party to the edge of the Rade de Brest. Here they found an uninhabited island and decided to settle. They built an oratory and cabins, and tried to work the soil for a vegetable garden. For three years they struggled here, enduring harsh weather, finding the earth unfruitful. Every day they looked across the expanse of water to what seemed an idyllic place, a river valley clad in thick forest. They watched the morning mist rise like smoke, and felt the powerful allure of such a peaceful place.*

After prayers one day St Guénolé asked his companions if they still had a desire to go there. They said it was up to him as the chosen one of God. He urged them to pray, then struck the shore with his staff. The waters parted, and, singing the hymn of Moses crossing the Red Sea, they walked across with dry feet.

St Guénolé

Unfortunately, their new settlement area lacked fresh water. St Guénolé prayed: "Jesus Christ, you who had the power to relieve the thirst of your followers in the desert, please grant this little band of monks a source of clear water." Then he traced his staff on the ground where a spring appeared.

One night, St Guénolé was praying in an oratory by the mouth of the river. Suddenly the Devil appeared to him in monster form, with eyes of flame and black feathers. The saint fearlessly admonished the beast, reminding it of the superior power of Christ. The evil vision disappeared. Another monk in a hut nearby overheard the whole thing and reported it to his companions.

St Guénolé was absolutely committed to an austere and devout lifestyle. He dressed only in goat-skin and had a stone for a pillow. He said fifty psalms three times a day and prayed constantly. He was always humble and kind to all, never miserable, nor angry, remaining gracious and serene at all times. He ate a simple diet of barley bread and vegetables, but no fat, and drank water mixed with apple juice. Often he fasted for days at a time.

As his fame spread far and wide, queues of those hopeful of healing grew — the blind, lame, deaf, lepers and those possessed by evil spirits. All wanted to lay eyes on the angelic face of this saint — in fact he was no longer a monk but like an angel among men.

* The beautiful site of St Guénolé's monastery is now Landévennec, where the river Aulne flows into the Rade de Brest. The ruins of a later medieval abbey remain (with an excellent museum) and there is a modern Benedictine abbey on the hillside above.

INTRODUCTION

Recumbent effigy of St Ronan (Locronan)

Tradition has it that Brittany is the land of a thousand saints. Stories of their exploits still circulate to this day and their legacy is physically present in cathedrals, country chapels, shrines, sacred springs and place-names. They were evangelists, miracle-workers and healers, on the cusp of legend and history. Some were regarded as the founders of Breton society, not only in terms of religious life but also in the origin of present-day towns and villages. Some are simply legendary and others have been confused through similarity of names. The arrival, reception and establishment of the saints have provided endless material for the oral tradition which is so strong in Brittany.

The Age of Saints saw arrivals from Great Britain over hundreds of years from the 5th century onwards to what would become Brittany (Little Britain). This was not exactly virgin territory, as there had already been plenty of contact between the two areas over a long period. It was not one movement or concerted effort but a piecemeal migration, small groups and individual religious leaders seeking to evangelise and to put down roots. The incomers settled in the west and along the north coast of Brittany, as place-names and the speaking of Breton indicate. Native born saints, including some from secular society, were also a product of this same often turbulent period. This was marked by power struggles in the political vacuum left by the end of Roman rule, and often called the Dark Ages for a lack of written evidence.

We know about the saints from occasional historical references, Lives or *Vitae* written by monks from the 9th century onwards and later collections of their deeds such as that by Albert Le Grand in 1637. A vast wealth of legendary material has also sprung up in almost every community. These Breton saints were human beings who lived among their people, often into very old age, not the early martyrs of the Catholic church. They have their status from popular acclaim through the centuries, and universal church values, rather than a formal Vatican sanction. People looked to them for help and guidance in everyday life, giving prayers and offerings in return. Anything from fair weather to marriage partners and good harvests might be requested, but if the relevant saint proved deaf to the plea, it was not unknown for a statue to be punished, even whipped with twigs... The relationship was close and personal.

This guide concentrates on a selection of Breton saints, with the historical context and some of the miracles and acts of healing which brought them fame and following. It also looks at flourishing aspects of their legacy today, such as the pardons, with processions and festivities still brimming with local pride and sense of community. A brief reference guide to official saints of the Catholic church with very popular cults in Brittany is also given, as well as an icon index, designed to help with identifying statues.

ORIGINS

St Cado (Île de St Cado)

Most of the Breton saints came originally from Great Britain and Ireland, often from religious establishments, such as the monastic school of St Ildut at Llanwit Major in Wales. St Pol, St Samson, St Gildas and St Brieuc were all pupils there. Ildut himself is a good example of conflicting traditions about the saints, with some believing he was born in Brittany and later travelled to Wales to found his monastery, and others that he was Welsh by birth. In Finistère, the town of Lanildut echoes his name, as does Loc-Ildut near Sizun.

Those leading the groups that came to Brittany were often already renowned for exceptional learning and powers that set them apart. As a boy of 10, St Brieuc performed his first miracle: when he was told off for losing an earthenware water pot (which he had given to a leper), a brass substitute appeared. When a flock of birds were eating all the abbey's newly planted seeds, St Pol made them follow him to the abbot to be punished.

Although many were already devoted to the religious life, the family background of the saints was often aristocratic. There are many stories of young men rejecting the more military ambitions of their parents and insisting on following a spiritual path. St Cado's father wanted him to lead an army but the young man ran away to a lonely hermitage to devote himself to God. St Pol's epithet Aurelian suggests that he came from the illustrious family of Ambrosius Aurelianus, a British warrior chieftain who fought the Anglo-Saxons. St Efflam was an Irish prince who fled to Brittany on the night of his wedding rather than abandon his convictions and vow of chastity.

Certainly the impetus of evangelism in an undeveloped land like Brittany was strong and motivated numerous monks to leave their religious houses and cross the Channel. St Pol is said to have had an angelic vision bidding him go and spread the word of God. Others were attracted by the solitude and wilderness for uninterrupted devotions.

The migrants brought their language with them and Breton would gradually develop from these Brythonic tongues mixed with the speech of the locals. Breton is closest to Cornish and Welsh in vocabulary and form, indicating the origins of the majority of settlers. Other Breton saints were direct descendants of these first arrivals. St Guénolé was the son of Fragan who came from Great Britain and settled where the town Ploufragan is now in Côtes d'Armor.

ARRIVALS

The saints travelled across the channel and arrived on the coasts of Armorica, as this area was then called, using the small craft of the time. The size of contingents varied from a saint travelling with a few companions to a group of a hundred in a little fleet of boats. It was a journey of about 24 hours in good weather. Famously the saints are said to have sailed miraculously in stone boats: **St Ronan** glided across from Ireland in this way, as did **St Budoc**. **St Conogan's** vessel (probably a fallen menhir) can still be seen near the Pointe du Millier. Such stories enhance the reputation of the saints as wonder-workers, and symbolise the incredible impact they would have on their new country, but the stone boat theory may be little more than a medieval scribal error confusing *cumba* (Latin for little boat) and *koum*, a valley or stone trough in old Breton.

Maen-Vag, a modern stone boat

The litter of oddly shaped stones on the shores of Brittany is another way of explaining why these stories developed. Many rocks are still pointed out today as the boat of this or that saint. In 2000, a seaworthy boat of granite, Maen-Vag, was constructed by Jean-Yves Menez and now stands outside Dol cathedral. Other legendary methods of transport included their own cloaks (**St Gildas**) or a raft made from leaves (**St Noyale**, see image on p.17). **St Malo** travelled some way with St Brendan on the back of a whale.

On arrival, the incomers' reception seems to have been generally positive, as connection between Great Britain and this area was already well-established. Riwal, lord of the northern area called Domnonée, initially sent armed men to destroy a party of newcomers and was struck by a seizure for his hostility. **St Brieuc** released him from this punishment, recognising his own cousin.

Some were accepted willingly after demonstrating their powers. **St Samson** provided miracle cures (see p.6) and was favoured with land in exchange. A few tales of ill-treatment on arrival may reflect localised hostility to the advent of migrant groups and individuals for religious or political reasons. The acquisition of land may have threatened the balance of the local economy and some secular leaders would not have wanted monks to acquire the influence that possession of territory and control of natural resources could bestow.

On the Côte de Goëlo, **St Ké** was taken for a demon, beaten by women with branches of gorse and left for dead on the shore, where his *fontaine* still stands. **St Herbot** was refused help or a place to settle, driven away aggressively to find a quieter spot. **St Ronan** was threatened after trying to stop wreckers on the coast of the Bay of Douarnenez and later accused of murdering the daughter of a female opponent. It would hardly be surprising if the arrival of strangers bringing a new way of life under a new religion aroused suspicion and wariness in the native population.

SETTLEMENT

The migrants from Great Britain found a sylvan landscape in western Brittany (later *Basse Bretagne*), sparsely populated and without sizeable centres of settlement. Things were different in eastern Brittany (or *Haute Bretagne*) where Rennes and Nantes were established towns from Roman times and the influence of the Roman Catholic church was authoritative. They hoped for grants of land from local land-owners on which to construct basic oratories for prayer and huts for dwellings. Here they would live the simple life of intense spirituality according to the principles of what is sometimes called 'Celtic Christianity', although this is a complex issue.

St Samson arrived in the Guyoult valley on the north coast and cured the wife (suffering from leprosy) and daughter (possessed by a demon) of Privatus, who then

Exorcism by St Samson (Dol cathedral)

offered the leader territory where Dol-de-Bretagne now stands. When the settlers were granted terrain, it was usually wild and wooded, requiring considerable labour to fell trees and clear the ground before building and farming. In the written *Lives* of the saints this act became a metaphor akin to 'a clean sweep' making way for the new religion and getting rid of the roots of paganism. The speed of St Brieuc's new development astonished the locals when they saw that 'what had been forest before was now occupied by the monks'. St Pol domesticated wild boar and a swarm of bees found on the site of St-Pol-de-Léon. Christianity was to be a transformative force. St Lunaire was led by a bird to a place where a few ears of wheat were already growing, and when his companions were daunted by the size of the task ahead, twelve stags appeared to offer their services for ploughing.

Once small communities were established, they soon attracted other people – in the long term, those providing services and supplies – so that villages very often formed around monastic units. Place-names today reflect these early origins of Brittany. *Plou/Plo/Plé* = parish (Ploumiliau, the parish of Miliau, etc.), *Loc and Lan/Lam* = holy place, hermitage (Lannedern, hermitage of Edern, Locquenolé, holy place of Guénolé, etc). This is a lasting tangible legacy of the Breton saints, perpetuating the idea of their role in the very foundation of Brittany, even though it would be centuries before such a political entity emerged. The pattern of these names shows that western Brittany and part of the north coast were the main areas they settled. (See map inside front cover.)

The battle of righteous faith was also to be fought in the landscape against paganism enshrined in natural sites worshipped by the Celts like rivers, hill-tops, trees and springs.

The latter were soon associated with the newcomers. Sacred springs today preserved as *fontaines* with stone surrounds were claimed to have been struck out of the earth by saints when water was needed to drink or to assuage wounds, as in the case of **St Ké** (see p. 5). This was held as another sign of their powers, even over nature.

Then there were the megaliths, monuments from the neolithic period, which were mistakenly attributed to the Druids. The common association of *menhirs* (standing-stones) and fertility, and of alignments with idolatrous rituals was fostered in later stories about the saints. **St Pol** (or **St Gildas**) is said to have driven out pagan priestesses from the stone circle on the eastern cliffs of the island of Ouessant. The famous huge *menhir* Men Marz (miracle stone) near Brignogan-Plage became a marker **St Pol** had placed to forbid the sea to encroach any further, thus usurping for Christianity whatever powers the stones were thought to possess in paganism. Many megaliths were much later Christianised by the addition of crosses and symbols of the new religion.

An echo of Christian imposition on earlier beliefs may lie in the *Tromenie* (journey around monastic territory). Famously celebrated in honour of **St Ronan** at Locronan to this day, a procession commemorates the circuit he regularly walked, said to trace the outline of an earlier Celtic *nemeton* (outdoor sacred space) based on the cosmological ideas of the Celts and their calendar, with twelve points marking their months, in Christian tradition transformed into stations of saints to be celebrated on the march. **St Thélo** also has his *Tromenie* at Landeleau, possibly based on earlier religious ritual. Like **St Edern**, he was allowed to establish his boundaries by riding a stag for the duration of one night to create the largest possible territory for the new settlement. Each is shown in this process in statuary (see front cover).

The saints also had many tussles with diabolic power. **St Cado** had difficulty building a bridge over the Etel to link Île-de-St-Cado with the mainland. The Devil did it in return for the first soul to cross, so the saint sent a cat over...

Finally, a story from the life of **St Goulven** illustrates the potential to be found in the agricultural richness of Brittany. He sent a follower named Maden to ask a neighbour for a gift. The man piled earth into the messenger's tunic, which became heavier and heavier as he struggled back to Goulven's hut. It had turned to gold, a symbol of the fecundity of northern Finistère, today a prime vegetable growing area.

St Goulven's gold (Goulven)

SEVEN FOUNDING SAINTS

The seven founding saints of Brittany are those that established the earliest 'cathedrals', all of which remain today in rather more sophisticated form than those first wooden structures: St-Pol-de-Léon (St Pol), Tréguier (St Tugdual), St Brieuc, St Malo, Dol-de-Bretagne (St Samson), Vannes (St Patern), Quimper (St Corentin). Of these men, five were incomers from Great Britain and two were first generation migrants, but the chronology of their lives and deaths cannot be given with any precision. Some are named in documents of early church councils, others remain elusive beyond the legends told of their miracles. They are thought to be at the heart of early parish organisation in their relevant areas. The **Tro Breiz** is a pilgrimage between the seven cathedrals, revived into modern form from a tradition which may go back to the Middle Ages, although the evidence is sketchy (see p.21). The Kreisker chapel in St-Pol-de-Léon contains these images of the founders.

St Corentin was a simple hermit in the 5th century on the slopes of the great hill of Menez Hom, living off water from a spring he had created by striking the earth with his staff, and a single fish which regenerated each time he threw it back into the pool. When King Gradlon arrived with a hunting party, the saint was able to feed them all in this way. After witnessing this miracle, the king asked Corentin to come back to Quimper with him and preside over the first cathedral.

    Symbol: fish, sometimes holding model of a cathedral building

St Pol or Paul Aurelien came from Wales and arrived on the island of Ouessant after a sea journey from Cornwall. He crossed to the mainland where place-names such as Lampaul-Plouarzel and Lampaul-Ploudalmézeau reflect his journey. There is also a tiny chapel at Prat Paol on the Aber Wrac'h. He met the local lord of the Île-de-Batz who gave him land and St Pol then dealt with a marauding dragon on the island, leading it like a dog to the edge of the sea. He reluctantly agreed to become bishop at what is now St-Pol-de-Leon, but preferred a contemplative life on the island.

    Symbol: dragon at his feet

St Tugdual (or more correctly Tudwal) has varying traditions, either arriving with St Brieuc or travelling across Finistère from Le Conquet before founding his monastery and later cathedral in what is now Tréguier in Côtes d'Armor. He is said to have visited Rome and been crowned pope after a dove settled on his shoulder, before miraculously returning to Brittany on a flying horse in a single night. From this story he is often called Pabu/Babu (= father).

    Symbol: dove on shoulder, pope's white mitre (hat)

St Brieuc founded the eponymous cathedral in the 5th century near the palace of his relative Riwal (see p.5). A story from later in his life tells how he was being carried in a litter by monks when a pack of wolves surrounded the travellers. His companions fled, but when the saint made the sign of the cross, the wild animals bowed down to him. This symbolises his programme of evangelisation, bringing sinners into the fold of the church.

Symbol: wolf or wolves

St Patern may have been born in Brittany but he had close connnections with Wales and spent some years there. His name appears in a document of the Council of Vannes held c465, perhaps the time when he was made bishop of that city. One story tells of a visit to Jerusalem, from which he returned with a golden cloak which was coveted by King Arthur. Local intrigues drove Patern out of Vannes and he died in the kingdom of Franks, but plague and famine hit his homeland as a punishment. In contrition, his bones were brought back and housed in a special church just outside the walled city, where he is honoured today, rather than at the nearby cathedral.

Symbol: model of his church

St Malo accompanied St Brendan on his voyages and came to the island of Cézembre off the coast of Brittany on the back of a whale. He founded a monastery on the mainland at Aleth, and performed many miracles, but was driven out by intrigue and jealousy, fermented by the Devil. He excommunicated his opponents before fleeing, and had to return later to lift this terrible punishment. In the 12th century the religious centre moved to what is now the town of St Malo and a new cathedral, now dedicated to St Vincent.

Symbol: whale

St Samson's name figures in a historical document recording those present at the Council of Paris in c550. He arrived in Brittany at the place where his *fontaine* stands today at Carfantin near Dol-de-Bretagne (see p.6). Building his cathedral attracted the jealousy of the Devil, who is said to have destroyed one tower, which has never been completed. In the 9th century Dol assumed great political signficance as Breton ruler Nominoë asserted the position of archbishop to be held here instead of recognising Tours, the official Catholic Metropolitan see, which was outside Brittany.

Symbol: archbishop's garb, including white pallium 'collar'

THREE MAJOR SAINTS

St Gildas (Gueltas in Breton) This saint came from Wales and is probably the author of *De excidio Britanniae,* a fiery 6th century diatribe against the moral corruption of Britain at the time of the Anglo-Saxon invasions. On arrival in Brittany he may have landed first on the north coast, where there is still a famous horse pardon each year on the Île St-Gildas near Bugélès. His most famous centre is Saint-Gildas-du-Rhuys on the Gulf of Morbihan, where a beautiful Romanesque church stands today. Just across the water is Île de Houat, his special place of isolated devotion and the site of his death.

Gildas also figures in the famous story of Conomor, as he replaced the severed head of Tréphine and brought her back to life (see p.11, 16). Near where this scene took place by the Blavet river is a remarkable troglodyte chapel dedicated to St Gildas.

Symbol: dog, pig, book

St Guénolé Son of an immigrant and brother of St Jacut, Guénolé was the founder of the beautiful abbey of Landévennec where medieval ruins stand today at the mouth of the Aulne on the Rade de Brest. At the famous monastic school of Budoc on Île Lavret, he healed the broken leg of one of his fellow pupils, a sign of divine gifts. Many miracles followed throughout his life, including the power of resurrection. He also parted the waters to walk dry-footed from Île Tibidy to the mainland. Guénolé became, like St Corentin, an important advisor of king Gradlon of Quimper, and he figured in the Breton Atlantis story. The city of Ys in the Bay of Douarnenez was flooded by the sea to punish the wickedness of Dahut, the king's daughter, and Guénolé persuaded Gradlon to throw his daughter from the horse carrying them to safety. In the waves she was transformed into the sea spirit Ahès.

Symbol: book, crozier, model of abbey

St Hervé (Houarneau in Breton) The son of a famous British bard, the saint was born blind so as 'not to see the vices of the world' as his mother had prayed. He is usually shown accompanied by a young boy, Guiharan, or a wolf as guide on his many travels around Brittany. The wolf had attacked the pair but then bowed down before Hervé and remained his constant companion. Hervé preferred a simple life based in a hermitage near Lanhouarneau to any church honours, but was highly respected everywhere for his wisdom and perception. The little chapel on top of Menez Bré in Côtes d'Armor is dedicated to St Hervé: this was the scene of the excommunication of Conomor (see page 11) in which he was involved. When a worldly official complained at waiting for a lowly monk, he was struck down paralysed, with unseeing eyes. Only St Hervé was able to revive him.

Symbol: shown in monk's robe, young guide, wolf

St Hervé (St-Anne-la-Palud)

NOBLE SAINTS

Not all saints were monks and priests. **Miliau** was a wise and devout local ruler in the 6th century, murdered by his brother Rivod in a power grab. His story is told in a painted altarpiece in the famous parish close at Guimiliau (= village of Miliau). It shows him beheaded, with his wife holding the severed head. In fact, it was his son **Mélar** (Méloir) who suffered this fate in the common tradition and his legend is very well-known.

Rivod feared the young man as a future rival and ordered his right hand and left foot to be cut off, so he would not be able to wield a sword or ride a horse. But a miracle occurred and Mélar grew a silver hand and bronze foot to compensate. His uncle then sent him away, but bribed his carer Kerialtan to assassinate the young man. Mélar's head was cut off and placed in a bag to be given to Rivod, but the killer was first struck blind, then dropped down dead, and Rivod died suddenly only a few days later. The church at Lanmeur, with its mysterious crypt where Mélar was buried, contains statues of the child martyr.

St Mélar mutilated (Lanmeur)

A contemporary tale describes the savage exploits of the tyrant Conomor, who is presented as the Breton Bluebeard, killing several wives in turn as they became pregnant to avoid the prophecy that his son would kill him. He finally married **Tréphine**, who was soon expecting a child. She ran away from her husband and gave birth to a son, **Trémeur,** but Conomor eventually found and killed her (see p. 16). St Gildas was able to bring her back to life, but little Trémeur was decapitated by his father and is shown in statuary holding his own head (a cephalophore saint). His church at Carhaix-Plouguer has a good example. Conomor was excommunicated by a gathering on the Menez Bré and later killed in battle by his step-son near the Abbaye du Relec.

The more historically documented 9th century saw the state of Brittany emerge as a political entity, with the efforts of Nominoë to unite the area against the Franks. His son Erispoë became king but was murdered by his cousin **Salomon**, whose expansionist policies during a fourteen year reign saw Brittany increase its territory into the Cotentin peninsula. He retired to a religious life – thus later a saint in popular tradition – but he in his turn was assassinated in 874 by his own son-in-law and the son-in-law of Erispoë. This may have happened at Plélan where he took refuge, but more probably Salomon travelled westwards to a monastery at what is now La Martyre where he met his fate. In the extraordinary church there a sumptuous statue with golden crown and armour also shows the dagger in the king's side.

SAINTS AND ANIMALS

Many legends tell of the early saints' encounters with certain beasts, which became their symbols in artistic representation. Later the same saints were called on by the population to protect their animals from harm. Prayers and offerings were made, and pardons (see p.20) often involved animal blessings.

Wild animals like dragons and wolves are used symbolically to represent the forces of paganism, so victorious saints were shown as saviours. **St Pol** rid the Île-de-Batz of a terrible monster (see p.8) and the same story is told of **St Armel**, usually shown in armour beneath his saint's cloak, and a dragon at the river Seiche near Rennes. His church is at Ploërmel. Armel was the favoured saint of Henry Tudor (once a semi-prisoner in Brittany) and has a statue near the king's tomb in Westminster Cathedral. Two knights, **St Néventer** and **St Derrien**, tried to convert the lord of La Roche Maurice by offering to get rid of a local dragon if he embraced Christianity. Irish prince **St Efflam** (see p.4) arrived in Brittany near Plestin-les-Grèves, where his chapel and *fontaine* can be seen by the shore. One day he came across King Arthur fighting a dragon at Grand Rocher. After miraculously providing a spring for the exhausted hero to drink, Efflam succeeded where brawn could not, calling out the dragon and commanding it to leap from the height.

St Envel (Loc-Envel)

Wolves are often shown as redeemable (hence symbolic of sinners), as in the stories of St Brieuc (p.9) and St Hervé (p.10). **St Thégonnec**, patron of the famous parish close, was bringing building stone for his oratory when a wolf attacked and killed the donkey pulling the cart. The saint commanded it to take the donkey's place. A tiny cart drawn by one of these animals became his symbol. **St Envel** was invoked against wolves (and to stop crows eating sown seeds). A stained glass window at Loc-Envel shows a domesticated wolf and stag working in the fields for the saint.

The stag was important in Celtic mythology and figures in many tales of the early saints. **St Edern** rides a stag on the calvary of his exquisite church in Lannédern. A traditional *gwerz* (song) in his honour tells how he arrived (from Ireland or Wales) with his sister, Jenovefa, and set up a simple hermitage. He kept a little cow which wandered onto the land of others. People complained and killed the cow, so Edern performed a miracle by reviving it. In fact the cow had left a trail of exceptionally fertile land wherever it grazed, perhaps a symbolic tale of failure to recognise the benefits of Christianity. The saint moved on to Lannédern. Here a stag being chased by hunters came to him for refuge. When he protected the animal, one of the lord's servants hit him across the face. The noble party were struck blind and immobile for their harsh treatment of the saint, until St Edern prayed for their release. His night ride on the stag is mentioned on page 7.

Horses have always been important in the history of Brittany. St Hervé and St Gildas were both equine patrons, the latter honoured to this day by a famous annual horse pardon, where riders and spectators walk out to the Île St-Gildas at low tide for mass at a tiny chapel and presentation of blessed bread to each animal. A horse festival is still held on the Menez Bré by St Hervé's chapel.

St Eloi (Alar), from Limousin but very popular in Brittany, was a blacksmith whose arrogance nearly led to disaster as he claimed to be 'Master of all'. One day a stranger came seeking work, and calmly cut off the foot of a waiting horse. Eloi was horrified, but the man put the horseshoe on the severed foot and then the foot back on its leg again without any suffering to the animal. Sending the stranger away, Eloi tried out this revolutionary method on another horse. As soon as he cut off the foot, the horse began to bleed and then collapsed, with Eloi powerless to put right what he had done. The stranger returned and restored the horse to health. He then walked away and Eloi saw a halo around his head: Christ himself had come to teach a lesson in humility.

Cattle came under the patronage of two contrasting saints: **St Cornely** in the south of the peninsula and **St Herbot** in the north. **Cornely** (whose name may echo the Latin *cornu* = horn) was pope in Rome in the 3rd century but had to flee persecution. Arriving near Carnac, Cornely was finally cornered by Roman soldiers and hid in the ear of a horned beast grazing on the plain. Another story says he prayed for divine aid and the soldiers were turned to stone, an explanation of the famous megaliths. The church

St Cornely and cattle (Carnac)

in Carnac is dedicated to him today and there is an annual blessing of horned beasts.

By contrast, **St Herbot** was an incomer from Great Britain. He settled in the Monts d'Arrée, first driven away from Berrien, and then given land and a choice of beasts by the lord of Rusquec, near the village of St-Herbot, which has a magnificent church and the saint's tomb. It was customary to leave hairs from cows' tails by the chancel. It was said he spoke the language of all horned beasts and could cure their ills. There is a *Fête de Beurre* (Butter Festival) every year in September.

St Jugon was a young shepherd who used to make a magic circle of protection round his sheep and cow when leaving them alone. One day he forgot and a wolf killed the cow, but Jugon revived it. He was accidentally killed by his uncle at the tender age of 16, later becoming a popular saint protector of sheep. Pigs get very little attention in popular tradition, coming under the auspices of **St Gildas** (and official Catholic saints St Nicodeme and St Antony), who also has an association with dogs (see p.15).

HEALING SAINTS

In the absence of doctors and powerful medicines, saints later became the focus of popular prayers for divine intervention in the face of illness. They performed miracles of healing in their life-times and posthumously often through the touching of their relics (usually armbones, fingers and skulls). Some dealt with one particular illness, others were more generalist. The sacred spring (*fontaine*) near the church or chapel was often the focus for healing rites.

St Cado's stone bed (Île de St Cado)

The association of particular issues with individual saints may be tenuous. When a goose plucked out the eye of Clervie, sister of **St Guénolé**, the saint extracted the organ from the animal's stomach and restored it to the girl, thus starting a reputation for curing eye problems. In a case of the blind curing the blind, **St Hervé** was efficacious. Water from the saint's *fontaine* was rubbed across the afflicted eye(s). For deafness and ear infections, the *fontaine* of **St Cado** was reputed to help. In his church on the Île de Saint Cado, there is a stone said to be the bed of the saint with an opening at the base for sufferers to place their heads for relief. The same goes for **St Urlou's** tomb at the Abbaye Sainte-Croix in Quimperlé. He is also called on for the relief of gout. **St Meriadec** cured deafness by placing a bell over the sufferer's head.

The ubiquitous problem of rheumatic pain in a humid Brittany naturally required the services of many saints. **St Guyomard** was invoked at a chapel in the commune of that name. A *menhir* inside the building was the focus for a healing ritual, with pilgrims rubbing their afflicted body part against it. **St They** was also called on to help with this malady at his little chapel with *fontaine* in dramatic surroundings on the Pointe du Van.

The chapel of Notre-Dame du Haut at Trédaniel celebrates the cult of seven healing saints, not all directly associated with Brittany, but covering problems with eyes, rabies, stomach pains, rheumatism, skin complaints and the pain of childbirth between them. One is **St Méen** who was well-known for curing skin disease, often called *mal de St Méen*. At what is St Méen-le-Grand today pilgrims came from far and wide to be healed of leprosy. **St Tugen** and **St Jacut** were also efficacious for this terrible disease. Jacut is said to have taken a leper's hand and thus cured the man, so his cult became a focus for the healing of this affliction.

St Maudez, who arrived at Port-Beni near Pleubian, washed an ulcerous wound on his arm in the local spring and was cured, so the *fontaine* of the saint became associated with the healing of skin diseases and boils. Soon St Maudez sought greater solitude and moved to the island now named after him – Île Modez. He is said to have cleared the land of snakes, so also became efficacious in the treatment of snake bites. Near Plouyé in Finistère a lonely countryside chapel to St Maudez has a pretty *fontaine* associated with the healing of eczema and shingles.

In the event of scabies, it was advised to soak a cloth in **Saint Meriadec's** *fontaine* and wrap yourself in it. This wetting of clothes with sanctified water and pressing them on wounds or sore limbs was a common ritual. It could be used when the patient was too ill to get to the chapel site themselves. The miraculous spring of **St Goulven** (see p.7) in the village of that name has a stone sarcophagus incorporated in the structure where pilgrims would lie in the hope of a cure. At the annual pardon, the priest would dip the sacred relic (arm-bone of St Goulven) into the water to sanctify it.

St Gildas' church at Magoar, well-known for its little bell-wheel, had a curious ceremony at the *fontaine* on the last Sunday in January. Dogs were brought to be blessed against succumbing to rabies, and they fed from a stone 'bowl' called the *Toul a hi* (dog hole). If bitten by a rabid dog, a tradition advised looking into the water: if you saw a dog reflected it was bad news, if not you had escaped the threat of rabies. The same process is recorded at the beautiful church and *fontaine* of **St Tugen** at Primelin.

Mental health also fell within the remit of the saints. In earlier times mental disturbances were thought to be the activity of malicious spirits or the Devil himself, and exorcism was practised. An illustration of **St Samson** extracting the evil spirit through the victim's head (see p.6) can be seen in Dol-de-Bretagne cathedral. **St Hervé** (see page 10), was a healer of fear and anxiety. Because he tamed a wolf, the blind saint was called on in cases of fear of wolves/weir-wolves and through this he became known for helping nervous anxiety and depression.

There really was no affliction without its patron, giving hope of improvement in almost all cases. Those with haemorrhoid problems should seek the services of **St Fiacre**, an Irish saint and famous gardener. At Radenac in Morbihan, he has a chapel and *fontaine*, which could also help with dysentery and abscesses. He was even invoked for syphilis.

And if all had failed, a final appeal, kill or cure, was made to **Diboan**, a name meaning deliverance, also called Abibon or Tu pe du ('from one side or another'). One method practised at Plévin was to light a candle to the saint: if it burned brightly the sufferer would survive, if it guttered there was no hope.

St Goulven's sacred spring (Goulven)

FEMALE SAINTS

The function of female saints was often to demonstrate chastity, piety and fidelity. Some literally lost their heads over their faith. Some had supporting roles to their menfolk, like **Scifolla** (sister of St Pol) who set up her own monastery. **Jenofeva** (Genevieve) tried to cheat her brother Edern out of land by making a cock crow to end his boundary ride early (see p.7). She does at least have a church dedicated to her at Loqueffret. There

St Tréphine beheaded (St-Tréphine)

are also the noblewomen with value as political pawns. **St Tréphine** (see page 11), daughter of the count of Vannes, unfortunate last wife of Conomor, managed to flee and hide with her young son for some years, but was finally beheaded by her relentless husband. Here was a woman of high birth used in a political marriage advantageous to her father despite the dubious reputation of her suitor.

St Haude (Aude) is a cephalophore (or head-carrying saint), associated with the evocative ruined Château de Trémazan. Her father's second wife made the children's lives unbearable, sending Haude's brother Tanguy away to court and treating Haude little better than a slave. Tanguy returned years later and believed false allegations of promiscuity against his sister, beheading her in punishment. Soon learning the truth of her virtue, the devastated Tanguy confronted his father and step-mother. Haude appeared with her head replaced on her shoulders, and by silent regard accused her step-mother before falling dead.

The wicked step-mother, that traditional motif of folklore, figures in other stories. A 13th century tower in the chateau of Brest is still called after **St Azenor**. She married the count of Goëlo, but when pregnant was accused of adultery by her father's second, jealous wife. She was shut up in the tower that bears her name and condemned to be burnt alive. When the flames did not touch her, she was put into a barrel and hurled into the sea. The waves carried Azenor to the shore of Ireland, where she gave birth to a son, Budoc, who would also become a saint.

A few women were able to pursue the quiet life of prayer they had envisaged on leaving their homeland. **St Enora** (Honora) followed Efflam (see p.4) from Ireland and landed in the Baie de la Vierge near Le Yaudet after being caught in a fishing net. When she refused to marry the local lord, he chased her to the Lieue de Grève where he was struck down by paralysis. Efflam cured the nobleman when he showed remorse. Enora had her own oratory near that of the man she had once hoped to marry and devoted herself to prayer. Each day she rang a bell which Efflam could hear in his own solitude, until one day there was only silence.

St Noyale (Nolwen), a princess from Cumbria, came to Brittany in the 6th century, travelling on a leaf, to avoid an arranged marriage. The commune of Noyal-Pontivy is a reminder of her story. She was pursued by a suitor who took rejection badly and cut off her head. In the tradition of cephalophores, she took this up and set off on her last walk. The location of *Trois fontaines* is where three drops of her blood fell to the ground. A large chapel now commemorates her final resting place.

St Noyale arriving (Sainte-Noyale)

The ideals of motherhood, later focused on the cult of the Virgin Mary, also figure in the pantheon of Breton saints with St **Guen** (Gwenn), the mother of three saints (Guénolé, Vennec and Jacut), shown in statuary as nursing the three babies with triple breasts, a miraculous gift from God. New mothers appeal to her for good, well-flowing milk, and cures for childhood eczema, using a garment soaked in her *fontaine* and applied to the infected area.

St Nonne (Non in Wales) mother of Saint David (Divy, Dewi in Wales), was also a patroness of nurselings and infants. Her help was sought by mothers of children slow to walk. She came to Brittany in the late 6th century from Wales after being raped and impregnated by the bard Caradec, and took refuge in the forests around Landerneau. She gave birth on a stone which is said to have taken the shape of a cradle. A spring which burst out from the earth for her to baptise the young Divy, is now a picturesque *fontaine* dedicated to the saint. There is another stone about 50m away also associated with St Nonne, with the indentations (cup marks) said to be those of her knees as she prayed. Offerings are still laid there to this day.

Of the traditional Catholic saints, **Notre-Dame** (the Virgin Mary) remains the most popular of all sacred figures in Breton churches, especially in her role as a protective mother. There are many local legends, such as that of Notre-Dame des Ronciers (brambles), patron of Josselin. A peasant found her statue in a bramble patch and took it home. The statue miraculously returned to its original place and so a chapel – now a basilica – was built on the spot.

St Marguerite is shown with a dragon at her feet and a cross in her hand – reflecting the tale that she was swallowed by the beast but escaped unharmed by tickling its innards with her crucifix. So with a pleasing irony, women prayed to this virgin saint that they would give birth as easily as she had emerged from the dragon's stomach.

Statues of **St Barbe** (or Barbara) hold a model tower, showing the place where she was imprisoned by her father after refusing to marry through devotion to her Christian faith. After he decapitated his daughter for her defiance, he was struck dead by a lightning bolt. St Barbe is now the patron of firemen. **St Apollonia**, a 3rd century martyr from Roman Egypt, holds a pair of pliers, denoting the torture she suffered by tooth extraction... She is of course the patron of dentists.

PATRON SAINTS

St Yves (Sant Erwan in Breton) and St Anne are the male and female patron saints of Brittany. Their images appear with great frequency in churches and chapels all over the region, and yet there could hardly be a greater contrast between the two: Yves, a well-documented historical individual, and Anne, a legendary figure from the life of Jesus who features not in the Gospels but only in later works of uncertain origin, the Apocrypha.

We know a great deal about Yves Hélory and his life in the late 13th century, and have the testimony of many who had direct contact with him. Anne is an unknown quantity, subject of conflicting and confusing stories, with nothing of certainty except the tradition that she was the mother of Mary and grandmother of Jesus. It speaks volumes of the open embrace of Breton faith that each has their honoured place in this land of saints.

St Yves, unlike the other earlier Breton saints, was actually officially canonised by the Catholic Church in 1347. He was born in 1253 at Minihy-Tréguier, adjoining the cathedral town of Tréguier. After local education, Yves went to university in Paris and Orleans. He

St Yves (St-Herbot)

returned to Rennes and then Tréguier as an ecclesiastical judge and advocate. He soon gained a reputation for defending the poor and favouring them in judgements. His later iconography often portrays the saint between a rich and poor petitioner, with his head inclined towards the latter.

He also became a priest and was given the coastal parish of Trédrez (1284-1292), where the paved way (*pavé*) he walked between presbytery and church can still be seen, and then Louannec, which was closer to his home at Minihy-Tréguier and to the nearby cathedral of Tréguier where he had many duties. Throughout his working life, Yves walked great distances to return to the family manor, where he had established a refuge for the poor and disabled. Indeed he was an indefatigable walker, sometimes preaching in seven different churches on one day. In the countryside he often stopped to preach at wayside crosses, speaking simply to the people in Breton. He was well-known for his very austere life, giving away all he had to the needy.

Yves was widely revered in his lifetime and after his death in 1303, many miracles were attested at his tomb in the cathedral at Tréguier. This was destroyed during the Revolution and later reconstructed. At Minihy-Tréguier his 'tomb' is an outdoor altar in the cemetery, through which pilgrims crawl on the day of the Pardon of St Yves, May 19th. This festival is attended by thousands today, including lawyers from many countries, as Yves is also the patron saint of this profession. The relic of his skull is carried from the cathedral to the church at Minihy-Tréguier in a grand procession.

St Anne is easily recognisable in church and chapel statuary: a tall, slender woman with veiled head (sometimes a crown), she is most often shown with a book, teaching the young Mary to read, an affecting mother and daughter portrayal. Occasionally her grandson Jesus makes a group of three. She is not precisely a Breton saint, although her cult has been very popular in Brittany for centuries. In the Apocryphal tradition, she was married to Joachim, and mother of the Virgin Mary. Some see in the cult of Saint Anne an adaptation of the Celtic reverence for the pagan goddess Ana.

St Anne (St-Anne-la-Palud)

St Anne is frequently identified (or confused) with Anne de Bretagne, duchess of Brittany in the late 15th century, much used as a symbol of 'Bretonness'.

There are many local traditions – particularly around the Bay of Douarnenez, where the church at Ste-Anne-La-Palud is famous – that she actually visited Brittany, in some versions with her young grandson Jesus in tow. Another tradition claims she was actually born here, and returned later in life where Jesus came to visit her, creating the spring that flows at the *fontaine* near the church. A famous Pardon is held here each year. Often Anne's story concerns domestic violence and her escape from a vicious husband either to Brittany from Judaea or vice versa before a better union with Mary's father Joachim.

At Commana the church of St Derrien, soberly fit for its setting in the stark hills of the Monts d'Arrée, conceals a rich interior containing the most spectacular of all memorials to Saint Anne, an elaborately gilded altarpiece from 1682. It presents Anne and Mary with a young Jesus flanked by pillared niches containing statues of Joachim and Joseph, their two husbands. A panel in the left corner presents the unusual scene of Anne in bed after the birth of her daughter and the midwife washing baby Mary whilst Joachim looks on.

The most elaborate shrine of St Anne is at Ste-Anne d'Auray, a vast 19th century monumental ensemble on the site of an earlier sanctuary. It is said that a local man, Yves Nicolazic, had visions of Anne from the summer of 1623. She told him to rebuild an ancient shrine in her honour. In March 1625 the light of a mysterious candle led Nicolazic to a field where a statue of Anne was found. The bishop of Vannes decided that a chapel should be built on this very spot. The original statue was destroyed at the time of the Revolution, with only a burnt fragment preserved and encased in the base of the current one which dates from 1825.

Today the great basilica of St Anne stands there, focus for thousands of pilgrims each year and actually recipient of a papal visit by Jean-Paul II in 1996. The annual Pardon on 26 July is a great spectacle with a statue of St Anne carried in procession through the park to the Memorial building, a monument in honour of the dead of WWI.

PARDONS

Attending a Pardon offers the chance to observe the continuing cult of saints in Brittany. The name suggests a time of forgiveness, reconciliation and the seeking of pardon for sins, and the practice goes back as far as the 15th century with a wide revival in the 19th. Today there are more than 1000 annual pardons. The event is an expression of community and shared values, as each saint's day is celebrated every year with a mass, procession and blessing, often followed by a *fest deiz* or *fest noz*, with music and dancing.

After the service, the procession is a form of pilgrimage, linear or circular, often directed to the *fontaine* or sacred spring, carrying the saint's relics and statues, banners and ceremonial crosses. Sometimes the sacred bones are dipped into the water to renew its powers of healing. Canticles in honour of the saint are sung, often in Breton, during the parade. Many wear traditional Breton costume in the unique style of the locality.

Despite common elements, each pardon has its own character, according to the saint concerned. At the cathedral town of Tréguier the skull of St Yves is brought 'home' to his native village for a short visit, at the village of St-Eloi, horses and donkeys are blessed, whilst boats of all kinds participate at the Pardon de la Mer in St-Malo. At Locronan the Grand Tromenie every six years sees the procession cover 12kms of countryside around the village (see p.7). Of the many pardons in honour of the Virgin Mary, the one held at the impressive basilica of Le Folgoët on the first weekend in September is a famous spectacle.

Some pardons associated with tiny country chapels are attended mainly by locals, for whom it is an important tradition and part of their heritage. Others are great public occasions attracting many thousands of visitors, as at St-Anne d'Auray each July, a two day event with torch-lit procession. All are symbolic of Brittany's vibrant heritage where faith has been a vital part of the fabric of social and historical identity.

Pardon of St Yves (Minihy-Tréguier)

The basic concept of the Pardon has even been adapted to modern life. In 1979 the first motorcyclist event was held at Porcaro in eastern Morbihan and is now an important ritual under the auspices of the Virgin Mary, '*La Madone des motards*'. A recent arrival is the popular camping-car pardon held at Malestroit at the end of August with a procession of vehicles and a blessing in the name of St Gilles, patron of the parish.

AND TODAY....

The world of the Breton saints is still very much alive today. The **Vallée des Saints** near Carnoët, created in 2009, is a cultural project on a vast scale, to promote Breton heritage connected with the saints. Here a hillside above the ancient chapel of St Gildas is gradually being covered with gigantic statues of individual saints, as imagined by modern sculptors using granite, the iconic stone of Brittany. Some statues have been created elsewhere, such as St Piran in Cornwall and St Dewi (David) in Wales, in keeping with the saints' origins, and brought across the channel, echoing the original journeys of the saints all those centuries ago. It is a remarkable spectacle and not to be missed. www.lavalleedessaints.com

St Efflam, Vallée des Saints

The **Tro Breiz** is a pilgrimage between the seven cathedrals of the seven founding saints: Quimper, St Pol, Tréguier, St Brieuc, St Malo, Dol-de-Bretagne, Vannes. This journey of over 600km was carried out, at least in part, from medieval times (where some historical reference is made to the Journey of the 'Sept saints') in fulfilment of a vow or as a penance. In recent times, the idea has been revived and there is an association devoted to creating and waymarking walking routes to cover each stage. Every year in August, there is an organised walk of one section, lasting a week. For details see www.tro.bzh

Finally, a modern twist on ancient practice shows the continuity of faith in the capacity of popular saints to help in everyday life. The flourishing shrine of **St Leonard** can be found beside the D175 near Andouillé Neuville in Ille-et-Vilaine. In the mid 19th century, Leonard was a local ne'er-do'well, a robber who used to block the tracks and break the wheels of farmers' carts. He decided to change his ways after observing the miracle of a bitter apple left in an oak tree turning sweet and juicy, a transformation from bad to good. He tried to help a traveller in trouble but was suspected of his old tricks and struck dead by a single blow. His tomb is on this spot, and now surrounded by an elaborate flowery shrine. Offerings of all sorts, often colour-coded in arrangement, are left in the grove of trees, photos and extremely personal objects, together with many dedicatory slate plaques giving thanks for wishes granted or asking for very specific help from the saint – to pass exams is a common plea, or find a job, have a baby, be cured of illness and many other heartfelt prayers reflecting modern life.

Tomb of St Leonard

All this testifies to the vibrancy and relevance of the Breton saints even in the busy world of the 21st century...

POPULAR CATHOLIC SAINTS

Statuary in churches and chapels often presents official saints of the Catholic Church, usually early martyrs or members of the Holy Family (especially Mary, Joseph and Jesus). Altars to **St Joseph**, who is shown holding Jesus by the hand, proliferated in the late 17th century after Louis XIV, who became a father for the first time in 1661, consecrated France to the saint. Another common subject for transept altars is the **Rosary**, showing the Virgin Mary giving rosary beads to St Catherine of Sienna and St Dominic, who had an apparition of Our Lady in 1214. The 15 Mysteries of the Rosary are shown in medallions around the main scene.

The 12 Apostles are to be seen in the porch of many churches. (Note: the order may vary and even the symbols, which are mostly the instruments of torture they suffered.)

Apostles (Bodilis)

   To the right: St Peter (key), St Andrew (saltire cross), St James (pilgrim's staff, hat with scallop shell), St John (cup with snake), St Matthew (scales, money-bag), James the Younger (club). **To the left**: Philip (T-shaped cross), St Simon (saw), St Bartholemew (flaying knife), Thomas (carpenter's square, axe), Thaddeus/Jude (cudgel), Matthias, who replaced Judas Iscariot (curved sword, bible).

St Anthony was an Egyptian monk in the 3rd century, regarded as a founder of monasticism. He is shown dressed in a monk's habit and often accompanied by a pig, and sometimes a little bell. (Not to be confused with St Anthony of Padua, early 13th century, the patron of lost things, shown in a Franciscan habit, holding a book and the infant Jesus, and sometimes a lily.)

St Laurent is very popular in Breton churches. A 3rd century victim of Roman persecution of Christians, he was roasted on a grill – his symbol in statuary – and famously told his torturers, 'You can turn me over now, this side's done'.

St Roch (early 14th century) can be seen in very many churches and chapels all over the region. He holds up his tunic to show a plague boil on his leg, and is usually accompanied by a little dog, sometimes carrying a loaf of bread. When St Roch contracted the plague after nursing the sick, he withdrew to the forest to die. A little dog brought him bread each day and he survived. There is a French expression *St Roch et son chien* to describe two people who are inseparable.

St Roch (St-Thégonnec)

St Sebastian was a 3rd century martyr, victim of the persecutions of Diocletian. He was pierced by many arrows, but did not die then. Healed of his wounds, he took the emperor to task for his sins and was clubbed to death.

INDEX A: SAINTS
(official Catholic saints in brackets)

INDEX B: ICONS

Use this index to identify the saint, then use index A to find his/her details.
Unfortunately some saints have the same symbol, but this list offers a basic starting
point with the commonest images of Breton/Catholic saints.

Icon - saint

Archbishop's mitre – St Samson
Armour – St Armel, St Néventer, St Derrien, Archangel Michael
Arrows – St Sebastian
Bell – St Meriadec
Bishop's mitre (hat) – St Pol, St Brieuc, St Tugdual, St Malo, St Samson, St Patern, St Corentin

Blacksmith's anvil – St Eloi
Building (church, cathedral) – St Corentin (Quimper), St Samson (Dol), St Patern (Vannes)
Cow – St Herbot, St Cornely
Dagger in side – St Salomon
Deer – St Gilles
Dog (with loaf) – St Roch
Dogs (2) – St Gildas
Donkey and cart – St Thégonnec
Dove – St Tugdual
Dragon – St Pol, St Armel, St Efflam, St Marguerite, Archangel Michael
Fish – St Corentin
Grill – St Laurent
Hand (severed) – St Mélar
Head (severed, young boy) – St Trémeur, St Mélar
Head (severed, woman) – St Tréphine, St Noyale, St Haude
Horse – St Eloi/Alar
Leaf (as raft) – St Noyale
Monk's habit – St Hervé, St Fiacre, St Herbot
Pallium (archbishop's white collar) – St Samson
Pig – St Gildas, St Antoine, St Nicodeme
Pliers – St Apollonia
Pope's mitre (hat) – St Tugdual
Rich man, poor man (between) – St Yves
Spade – St Fiacre
Stag – St Edern, St Thélo, St Envel
Tall woman with veiled head (teaching little girl from book) – St Anne
Tower – St Barbe (Barbara)
Tunic raised to show boil – St Roch
Whale – St Malo
Wolf – St Hervé
Wolves – St Brieuc
Young boy companion – St Hervé (if with blind man), St Roch